BREAD MACHINE COOKBOOK

1200 DAYS OF EASY-TO-FOLLOW HANDS-OFF RECIPES UNLOCK THE FULL POTENTIAL OF YOUR BREAD MACHINE AND PREPARE PERFECT HOMEMADE BREAD

Poula Ray

Table of Contents

1. Introduction

This is a great cookbook for beginners because it will teach you how to use a bread machine to make delicious bread. It will explain the basic settings and cycles of most popular bread-making machines, as well as include recipes for savory and sweet breads, whole wheat bread, focaccia, pizza crust, and more. Each recipe also contains nutrition facts and prep and cooking times, making it perfect for first-time home bakers.

While a bread machine is great for making quick breads, you'll probably want to try baking some "rustic" bread from scratch once in a while. There are several types of bread recipes, including a selection of Italian focaccia. A bread machine is a great way to make bread, and using a bread machine makes baking easy and convenient. These recipes are easy to follow and use only a small amount of ingredients. In addition, they don't require any hands-on work on your part. For example, all you have to do is measure ingredients and put them into the bread maker. In the morning, you'll have fresh, hot bread to eat.

A bread machine will remove the task of kneading bread and making it rise. With a bread machine, you don't have to wait several hours for your bread to rise. The bread machine lets you make delicious, homemade bread in less than an hour.

You need a bread machine to use these recipes because they all call for a bread machine to make the bread. There are several bread machines on the market, and each one works differently. But don't let this scare away someone who wants to make bread with a bread machine. The recipes in this book tell you exactly what settings you need and how long the bread machine should be set at the different settings. A bread maker will make the preparation of bread very easy for you.

Chapter 1:   Breakfast Recipes

Recipe 1:   Amish Bread

Serving Size: 12

Cooking Time: 4 hours 10 minutes

Ingredients:

- 2 ¾ cups of bread flour
- ¼ cup canola oil
- 1 teaspoon active dry yeast
- ¼ cup white sugar
- ½ teaspoon salt
- 18 tablespoons warm water

Directions:

1. Add all the ingredients into the pan in the recommended order. Select Classic/White Bread cycle and press Start.
2. When the dough has raised and the second cycle of kneading is started, switch it off. Then start it again by resetting it. The dough will get 2 complete raising cycles before the final 1 before baking.

Nutritional Value: Calories 164; Fat 5.89g; Carbohydrates 23.4g; Protein 4.02g

Recipe 2: Apple Oatmeal Bread

Serving Size: 12

Cooking Time: 3 hours

Ingredients:

- 2 ¾ cups bread flour
- 2 teaspoon instant yeast
- 1 ½ teaspoon cinnamon
- ¼ cup ground flax
- 1/3 cup quick oats
- 3 tablespoon brown sugar
- 2/3 cup apple, peeled & diced
- 2 tablespoon vegetable oil
- 1 teaspoon vanilla
- 2/3 cup water
- 1/3 cup milk
- 1 ½ teaspoon salt

Directions:

1. Add all the prepared ingredients to the bread machine pan in the order recommended by your bread machine manufacturer.
2. Set bread machine to the basic bread cycle with a light crust.
3. Once your bread is done, remove it from the bread machine pan and let it cool completely.
4. Slice and serve.

Nutritional Value: Calories 165; Fat 3.6g; Carbohydrates 28.9g; Protein 4.3g

Recipe 3: Buttermilk Bread

Serving Size: 12

Cooking Time: 4 hours 10 minutes

Ingredients:

- 3 cups all-purpose flour
- 2 teaspoon yeast
- 3 tablespoon sugar
- 2 tablespoon butter, unsalted & softened
- 1 ¼ cups warm buttermilk
- 1 teaspoon salt

Directions:

1. Add all the prepared ingredients to the bread machine pan in the order recommended by your bread machine manufacturer.
2. Set bread machine to the basic bread cycle with a light crust.
3. Once your bread is done, remove it from the bread machine pan and let it cool completely.
4. Slice and serve.

Nutritional Value: Calories 154; Fat 2.5g; Carbohydrates 28.3g; Protein 4.4g

Recipe 4: Cinnamon Applesauce Bread

Serving Size: 8

Cooking Time: 3 hours

Ingredients:

- 2 ½ cups bread flour
- 1 ½ teaspoon active dry yeast
- 1 tablespoon butter, unsalted
- 2 tablespoon brown sugar
- 1 tablespoon cinnamon
- ¾ cup buttermilk
- 1/3 cup applesauce
- 1 teaspoon salt

Directions:

1. Add all the prepared ingredients to the bread machine pan in the order recommended by your bread machine manufacturer.
2. Set bread machine to the white bread cycle with a light crust.
3. Once your bread is done, remove it from the bread machine pan and let it cool completely.
4. Slice and serve.

Nutritional Value: Calories 181; Fat 2.1g; Carbohydrates 35.3g; Protein 5.2g

Recipe 5: Coconut Almond Flour Bread

Serving Size: 12

Cooking Time: 55 minutes

Ingredients:

- 6 eggs
- 1 tablespoon butter, melted
- 1 tablespoon coconut oil, melted
- 1 teaspoon baking soda
- 2 tablespoon ground flaxseed
- 1 ½ tablespoon psyllium husk powder
- 5 tablespoon coconut flour
- 1 ½ cups almond flour

Directions:

1. Add all the prepared ingredients to the bread machine pan in the order recommended by your bread machine manufacturer.
2. Set bread machine to the quick bread cycle with medium crust.
3. Once your bread is done, remove it from the bread machine pan and let it cool completely.
4. Slice and serve.

Nutritional Value: Calories 106; Fat 7.2g; Carbohydrates 6.3g; Protein 4.6g

Recipe 6: Cornmeal Bread

Serving Size: 16

Cooking Time: 3 hours 5 minutes

Ingredients:

- 1 egg, beaten
- 3 cups bread flour
- 1 cup yellow cornmeal
- 2 ½ teaspoon dry yeast
- 1 1/3 tablespoon sugar
- 1 ½ cups water
- 1 teaspoon salt

Directions:

1. Add all the prepared ingredients to the bread machine pan in the order recommended by your bread machine manufacturer.
2. Set bread machine to the basic bread cycle with medium crust.
3. Once your bread is done, remove it from the bread machine pan and let it cool completely.
4. Slice and serve.

Nutritional Value: Calories 122; Fat 0.8g; Carbohydrates 25g; Protein 3.6g

Recipe 7: Country White Bread

Serving Size: 8

Cooking Time: 45 minutes

Ingredients:

- 2 teaspoons active dry yeast
- 1 ½ tablespoon sugar
- 4 cups bread flour
- 1 ½ teaspoon salt
- 1 large egg
- 1 ½ tablespoon butter
- 1 cup warm milk, with a temperature of 110°F to 115°F (43°C to 46°C)

Directions:

1. Put all the liquid ingredients in the pan. Add all the dry ingredients, except the yeast. Use your hand to form a hole in the middle of the dry ingredients. Put the yeast in the hole.
2. Secure the pan in the chamber and close the lid. Choose the basic setting and your preferred crust color. Press Start.
3. Once done, transfer the baked bread to a wire rack. Slice once cooled.

Nutritional Value: Calories 105; Fat 10g; Carbohydrates 0g; Protein 12g

Recipe 8: Cracked Wheat Bread

Serving Size: 16

Cooking Time: 2 hours 10 minutes

Ingredients:

- 1 ¼ cups whole wheat flour
- 2 ¼ teaspoon active dry yeast
- ½ cup cracked wheat
- 2 ¼ cups bread flour
- 2 tablespoon honey
- 1 ½ tablespoon butter
- 11 oz water
- 1 ½ teaspoon salt

Directions:

1. Add all the prepared ingredients to the bread machine pan in the order recommended by your bread machine manufacturer.
2. Set bread machine to the white bread cycle with medium crust.
3. Once your bread is done, remove it from the bread machine pan and let it cool completely.
4. Slice and serve.

Nutritional Value: Calories 123; Fat 1.4g; Carbohydrates 24.2g; Protein 13.2g

Recipe 9: Cranberry Almond Bread

Serving Size: 8

Cooking Time: 3 hours

Ingredients:

- 2 cups bread flour
- 1 ½ teaspoon quick rise yeast
- 1 tablespoon butter, unsalted
- 3 tablespoon slivered almonds
- ¼ cup dried cranberries
- 1 tablespoon sugar
- 1/3 cup dried apricots, chopped
- 1 cup water
- 1 teaspoon salt

Directions:

1. Add all the prepared ingredients to the bread machine pan in the order recommended by your bread machine manufacturer.
2. Set bread machine to the white bread cycle with medium crust.
3. Once your bread is done, remove it from the bread machine pan and let it cool completely.
4. Slice and serve.

Nutritional Value: Calories 155; Fat 2.9g; Carbohydrates 27.6g; Protein 4.3g

Recipe 10: Cranberry Bread

Serving Size: 16

Cooking Time: 3 hours

Ingredients:

- 4 cups bread flour
- 2 teaspoon bread machine yeast
- ¾ cup pecans, toasted & chopped
- 1 cup dried cranberries
- 2 tablespoon milk powder
- ¼ cup sugar
- 2 tablespoon butter, unsalted
- 1 ¼ cups + 2 tablespoon water
- 1 ½ teaspoon salt

Directions:

1. Add all the prepared ingredients to the bread machine pan in the order recommended by your bread machine manufacturer.
2. Set bread machine to the white bread cycle with medium crust.
3. Once your bread is done, remove it from the bread machine pan and let it cool completely.
4. Slice and serve.

Nutritional Value: Calories 152; Fat 2.2g; Carbohydrates 28.4g; Protein 3.9g

Recipe 11: Flax and Sunflower Seed Bread

Serving Size: 8

Cooking Time: 25 minutes

Ingredients:

- 1 ⅓ cups water
- 2 tablespoons butter softened
- 3 tablespoons honey
- 2/3 cups of bread flour
- 1 teaspoon salt
- 1 teaspoon active dry yeast
- ½ cup flax seeds
- ½ cup sunflower seeds

Directions:

1. With the manufacturer's suggested order, add all the ingredients (apart from sunflower seeds) to the bread machine's pan.
2. The select basic white cycles and press start.
3. Just in the knead cycle that your machine signals alert sounds, add the sunflower seeds.

Nutritional Value: Calories 140; Fat 4.2g; Carbohydrates 22.7g; Protein 4.2g

Recipe 12: Gingerbread Oat Bread

Serving Size: 16

Cooking Time: 3 hours

Ingredients:

- 3 cups bread flour
- ¼ oz active dry yeast
- ¼ teaspoon ground cloves
- ¼ teaspoon ground nutmeg
- ½ teaspoon orange zest, grated
- 1 ½ teaspoon ground ginger
- 1 ½ teaspoon ground cinnamon
- 1 cup old-fashioned oats
- 1 tablespoon vegetable oil
- ½ cup molasses
- 1 cup + 1 tablespoon warm water
- 1 teaspoon salt

Directions:

1. Add all the prepared ingredients to the bread machine pan in the order recommended by your bread machine manufacturer.
2. Set bread machine to the basic bread cycle with medium crust.
3. Once your bread is actually done, remove it from the bread machine pan and let it cool completely.
4. Slice and serve.

Nutritional Value: Calories 144; Fat 1.5g; Carbohydrates 29.5g; Protein 3.3g

Recipe 13: Honey Sesame Bread

Serving Size: 8

Cooking Time: 25 minutes

Ingredients:

- ¼ cups water
- ¼ cup honey
- 1 tablespoon powdered buttermilk
- 1 ½ teaspoons salt
- 3 Cups bread flour
- 3 tablespoons wheat bran
- ½ cup sesame seeds, toasted
- ¼ teaspoons active dry yeast

Directions:

1. Into the bread machine's pan, place all the ingredients by following the order endorsed by your machine's manufacturer.
2. Set the mechanism to the Basic Bread cycle.

Nutritional Value: Calories 62; Fat 3.1g; Carbohydrates 8.4g; Protein 1.7g

Recipe 14: Keto Breakfast Bread

Serving Size: 16

Cooking Time: 40 minutes

Ingredients:

- ½ teaspoon xanthan gum
- ½ teaspoon salt
- 2 tablespoons coconut oil
- ½ cup butter, melted
- 1 teaspoon baking powder
- 2 cups of almond flour
- 7 eggs

Directions:

1. Preheat the oven to 355F.
2. Beat eggs in a bowl on high for 2 minutes.
3. Add coconut oil and butter to the eggs and continue to beat.
4. Line a loaf pan with baking paper and pour the beaten eggs.
5. Pour in the rest of the ingredients and mix until it becomes thick.
6. Bake until a toothpick comes out dry, about 40 to 45 minutes.

Nutritional Value: Calories 234; Fat 23g; Carbohydrates 1g; Protein 7g

Recipe 15: Keto Coconut Bread

Serving Size: 8

Cooking Time: 1 hour 30 minutes

Ingredients:

- ½ cup coconut flour
- ½ cup ground flaxseed
- 2 tablespoons no-calorie sweetener of your choice
- 1 tablespoon baking powder
- 1 teaspoon xanthan gum
- ½ teaspoon ground cinnamon
- ½ teaspoon salt
- 6 eggs
- 1/3 cup coconut milk
- 1/3 cup coconut oil

Directions:

1. Put all the wet ingredients first into the bread pan before adding the dry ingredients.
2. Press the "Quick" or "Cake" setting of your bread machine.
3. Remove the pan from the machine once all cycles are finished.
4. Keep the bread in the pan for 10 more minutes.
5. Take the bread out of the pan to cool down.
6. Slice and serve.

Nutritional Value: Calories 122; Fat 9g; Carbohydrates 4g; Protein g

Recipe 16: Mozzarella Tomato Bread

Serving Size: 8

Cooking Time: 2 hours 35 minutes

Ingredients:

- 2 cups bread flour
- 2 teaspoon dry yeast
- 1 tablespoon sun-dried tomato, crumbled
- 1 cup mozzarella cheese, shredded
- 1 tablespoon milk powder
- 1 tablespoon butter, unsalted
- 1 tablespoon basil, minced
- 2 tablespoon sugar
- 2 tablespoon dehydrated onions
- 1 cup water
- 1 teaspoon salt

Directions:

1. Add all the prepared ingredients to the bread machine pan in the order recommended by your bread machine manufacturer.
2. Set bread machine to the white bread cycle with a light crust.
3. Once your bread is done, remove it from the bread machine pan and let it cool completely.
4. Slice and serve.

Nutritional Value: Calories 161; Fat 2.6g; Carbohydrates 29.2g; Protein 5.2g

Recipe 17: Mushroom and Leek Bread

Serving Size: 8

Cooking Time: 3 hours

Ingredients:

- 2 tablespoons butter
- 2 cups sliced mushrooms Portobello preferred
- 3/4 cup sliced leeks
- 1 1/2 teaspoon dried thyme
- 1 1/3 cups water
- 1 1/2 teaspoon salt
- 2 tablespoons liquid honey
- 1 1/4 cups whole wheat flour
- 3 cups all-purpose flour or bread flour
- 1 teaspoon bread machine yeast

Directions:

1. In a large-sized saucepan, heat butter over medium-high heat. Add mushrooms, leeks, and thyme; sauté just until tender. Immediately place in baking pan.
2. Measure remaining ingredients into the baking pan in the order recommended by the manufacturer. Insert pan into the oven chamber.
3. Select Basic Cycle.

Nutritional Value: Calories 130; Fat 5g; Carbohydrates 16g; Protein 8g

Recipe 18: Orange Cinnamon Bread

Serving Size: 12

Cooking Time: 3 hours

Ingredients:

- 1 egg
- 2 ½ cups bread flour
- 1 tablespoon orange zest
- ¼ cup maple syrup
- 1 tablespoon cinnamon
- ¾ cup milk
- ¼ cup raisins
- 1 ½ teaspoon yeast
- 2 tablespoon butter

Directions:

1. Add all the ingredients except raisins to the bread machine pan in the order recommended by your bread machine manufacturer.
2. Set bread machine to the basic bread cycle with medium crust.
3. When the machine beeps, add the raisins.
4. Once your bread is done, remove it from the bread machine pan and let it cool completely.
5. Slice and serve.

Nutritional Value: Calories 154; Fat 2.9g; Carbohydrates 28.2g; Protein 4g

Recipe 19: Orange Date Bread

Serving Size: 8

Cooking Time: 1 hour 30 minutes

Ingredients:

- 2 cups all-purpose flour
- 1 cup dates, chopped
- ¾ cup sugar
- ½ cup walnuts, chopped
- 2 tablespoons orange rind, grated
- 1 ½ teaspoons baking powder
- 1 teaspoon baking soda
- ½ cup orange juice
- ½ cup water
- 1 tablespoon vegetable oil
- 1 teaspoon vanilla extract

Directions:

1. Put the wet ingredients then the dry ingredients into the bread pan.
2. Press the "Quick" or "Cake" mode of the bread machine.
3. Allow all cycles to be finished.
4. Remove the pan from the machine, but keep the bread in the pan for 10 minutes more.
5. Take the bread out of the pan, and let it cool down completely before slicing.

Nutritional Value: Calories 80; Fat 2g; Carbohydrates 14g; Protein 1g

Recipe 20: Pepperoni Bread

Serving Size: 10

Cooking Time: 3 hours 10 minutes

Ingredients:

- 1 cup plus 2 tablespoons warm water
- 1/3 cup mozzarella cheese, shredded
- 2 tablespoons sugar
- 1 1/2 teaspoons garlic salt
- 1 1/2 teaspoons dried oregano
- 3 1/4 cups bread flour
- 1 1/2 teaspoons active dry yeast
- 2/3 cup sliced pepperoni

Directions:

1. Add the first six ingredients in order listed above, reserving the yeast.
2. Make a well in the flour; pour the yeast into the hole.
3. Select Basic bread setting, medium crust color, and press Start.
4. Check dough after 5 minutes of mixing and add 1 to 2 tablespoons of water or flour if needed. Just before the final kneading, add the pepperoni.
5. Remove loaf when finished and allow to cool for 10 to 15 minutes on a cooling rack before serving.

Nutritional Value: Calories 165; Fat 1.8g; Carbohydrates 34.1g; Protein 4.9g

Recipe 21: Rosemary Bread

Serving Size: 14

Cooking Time: 2 hours 10 minutes

Ingredients:

- 3 eggs
- ½ cup fresh rosemary, chopped
- ½ teaspoon xanthan gum powder
- 2 tablespoon monk fruit sweetener
- 1 ¼ cups vital wheat gluten
- ¾ cup oat fiber
- 2/3 cup almond flour
- 2/3 cup flaxseed meal
- 3 tablespoon olive oil
- 2 teaspoon rapid rise dry yeast
- 1 cup warm water
- 1 ½ teaspoon kosher salt

Directions:

1. Add all the prepared ingredients to the bread machine pan in the order recommended by your bread machine manufacturer.
2. Set bread machine to the basic bread cycle with medium crust.
3. Once your bread is done, remove it from the bread machine pan and let it cool completely.
4. Slice and serve.

Nutritional Value: Calories 127; Fat 6.7g; Carbohydrates 7.6g; Protein 10.3g

Recipe 22: Rosemary Cranberry Pecan Bread

Serving Size: 14

Cooking Time: 3 hours

Ingredients:

- 1 1/3 cups water, Plus
- 2 tablespoons water
- 2 tablespoons butter
- 2 teaspoons salt
- 4 cups bread flour
- ¾ cup dried sweetened cranberries
- ¾ cup toasted chopped pecans
- 2 tablespoons non-fat powdered milk
- ¼ cup sugar
- 2 teaspoons yeast

Directions:

1. Add each ingredient to the bread machine in the order and at the temperature recommended by your bread machine manufacturer.
2. Close the lid, select the basic bread, medium crust setting on your bread machine, and press start.
3. When the bread machine has finished baking, remove the bread and put it on a cooling rack.

Nutritional Value: Calories 120; Fat 5g; Carbohydrates 18g; Protein 9g

Recipe 23: Rosemary Sun-Dried Tomato Bread

Serving Size: 20

Cooking Time: 3 hours 40 minutes

Ingredients:

- 3 ¾ cups bread flour
- 1 ¼ teaspoon bread machine yeast
- ½ teaspoon paprika
- 1 teaspoon dried rosemary, crushed
- 2 tablespoon sugar
- 2 tablespoon vegetable oil
- 1/3 cup sun-dried tomatoes, cut into julienne
- 1 ¼ cups warm water
- 1 teaspoon salt

Directions:

1. Add all the prepared ingredients to the bread machine pan in the order recommended by your bread machine manufacturer.
2. Set bread machine to the basic bread cycle with medium crust.
3. Once your bread is done, remove it from the bread machine pan and let it cool completely.
4. Slice and serve.

Nutritional Value: Calories 103; Fat 1.6g; Carbohydrates 19.4g; Protein 2.6g

Recipe 24: Russian Rye Bread

Serving Size: 12

Cooking Time: 3 hours

Ingredients:

- 1 1/4 cups warm water
- 1 3/4 cups rye flour
- 1 3/4 cups whole wheat flour
- 2 tablespoons malt (or beer kit mixture)
- 1 tablespoon molasses
- 2 tablespoons white vinegar
- 1 teaspoon salt
- 1/2 tablespoon coriander seeds
- 1/2 tablespoon caraway seeds
- 2 teaspoons active dry yeast

Directions:

1. Mix the prepared dry ingredients together in a bowl, except for yeast.
2. Add wet ingredients to bread pan first; top with dry ingredients.
3. Make a well in the actual center of the dry ingredients and add the yeast.
4. Press Basic bread cycle, choose medium crust color, and press Start.
5. Remove from the prepared bread pan and allow to cool on a wire rack before serving.

Nutritional Value: Calories 141; Fat 0.8g; Carbohydrates 29.7g; Protein 5g

Recipe 25: Simple Potato Bread

Serving Size: 10

Cooking Time: 3 hours

Ingredients:

- 3 cups bread flour
- 2 teaspoon bread machine yeast
- 1 tablespoon sugar
- ½ cup instant potato flakes
- 2 tablespoon canola oil
- ½ cup warm water
- ¾ cup warm milk
- 1 ½ teaspoon salt

Directions:

1. Add all the prepared ingredients to the bread machine pan in the order recommended by your bread machine manufacturer.
2. Set bread machine to the basic bread cycle with a light crust.
3. Once your bread is done, remove it from the bread machine pan and let it cool completely.
4. Slice and serve.

Nutritional Value: Calories 186; Fat 3.6g; Carbohydrates 33g; Protein 5g

Recipe 26: Spinach and Feta Whole Wheat Bread

Serving Size: 8

Cooking Time: 25 minutes

Ingredients:

- 2/3 cups whole wheat flour
- 1 1/2 teaspoon instant yeast
- 1/4 cup unsalted butter, melted
- 1 cup lukewarm water
- tablespoon sugar
- 1/2 teaspoon salt
- 3/4 cups blanched and chopped spinach, fresh
- 1/2 teaspoon pepper
- 1/2 teaspoon paprika
- 1/3 cup feta cheese, mashed

Directions:

1. Preparing the ingredients. Place all ingredients, except spinach, butter, and feta, in the bread pan in the liquid-dry-yeast layering.
2. Put the pan in the Zojirushi bread machine.
3. Select the Bake cycle. Choose Regular Whole Wheat. Press start.
4. When the dough has gathered, manually add the feta and spinach.
5. Resume and wait until the loaf are cooked. Once cooked, brush with butter.
6. The machine will start the keep warm mode after the bread is complete.
7. Make it stay in that mode for about 10 minutes before unplugging.
8. Remove the pan and just cool it down for about 10 minutes.

Nutritional Value: Calories 111; Fat 21g; Carbohydrates 6g; Protein 28g

Recipe 27: Sweet Milk Bread

Serving Size: 12

Cooking Time: 3 hours

Ingredients:

- 3 1/3 cups bread flour
- 1 tablespoon butter, unsalted & melted
- 2 teaspoon yeast
- ½ cup sweetened condensed milk
- 1 cup water
- 1 teaspoon salt

Directions:

1. Add all the prepared ingredients to the bread machine pan in the order recommended by your bread machine manufacturer.
2. Set bread machine to the basic bread cycle with medium crust.
3. Once your bread is done, remove it from the bread machine pan and let it cool completely.
4. Slice and serve.

Nutritional Value: Calories 178; Fat 2.4g; Carbohydrates 33.7g; Protein 4.9g

Recipe 28: Sweet Potato Bread

Serving Size: 10

Cooking Time: 3 hours

Ingredients:

- 4 cups bread flour
- 1 cup sweet potatoes, mashed
- ½ cup brown sugar
- 2 teaspoons yeast
- 1 ½ teaspoon salt
- ½ teaspoon cinnamon
- ½ cup water
- 2 tablespoons vegetable oil
- 1 teaspoon vanilla extract

Directions:

1. Add the prepared wet ingredients first then the dry ingredients to the bread pan.
2. Use the "Normal" or "Basic" mode of the bread machine.
3. Select the light or medium crust color setting.
4. Once the cycles are finished, take out the bread from the machine.
5. Cool down the bread on a wire rack before slicing and serving.

Nutritional Value: Calories 111; Fat 2g; Carbohydrates 21g; Protein 3g

Recipe 29: Tomato Onion Bread

Serving Size: 12

Cooking Time: 3 hours 50 minutes

Ingredients:

- 2 cups all-purpose flour
- 1 cup whole meal flour
- ½ cup warm water
- 4 3/4 ounces (140 ml) milk
- 3 tablespoons olive oil
- 2 tablespoons sugar
- 1 teaspoon salt
- 2 teaspoons dry yeast
- ½ teaspoon baking powder
- 5 sun-dried tomatoes
- 1 onion
- ¼ teaspoon black pepper

Directions:

1. Prepare all the necessary products. Finely chop the onion and sauté in a frying pan. Cut up the sun-dried tomatoes (10 halves).
2. Pour all liquid ingredients into the bowl; then cover with flour and put in the tomatoes and onions. Pour in the yeast and baking powder, without touching the liquid.
3. Select the baking mode and start. You can choose the Bread with Additives prog, and then the bread maker will knead the dough at low speeds.

Nutritional Value: Calories 121; Fat 10g; Carbohydrates 6g; Protein 28g

Recipe 30: White Bread

Serving Size: 12

Cooking Time: 3 hours

Ingredients:

- 1 cup warm water 110°F
- 1 (.25 ounce) OR (2 ½ teaspoons) package bread machine yeast
- ¼ cup vegetable oil
- 3 cups bread flour
- 1 teaspoon salt
- Sugar

Directions:

1. In the bread machine, place the water, sugar and yeast.
2. Dissolve the yeast for 10 min.
3. Add the oil, flour and salt to this foamy yeast.
4. Select the actual Basic or White Bread setting and press Start.
5. Serve when cool.

Nutritional Value: Calories 163; Fat 5.11g; Carbohydrates 25.8g; Protein 4.1g

Chapter 2:   Lunch Recipes

Recipe 31: Apple Nut Bread

Serving Size: 12

Cooking Time: 3 hours 10 minutes

Ingredients:

- 1 egg
- 8 oz apple juice
- 4 cups bread flour
- 2 teaspoon active dry yeast
- ½ teaspoon baking soda
- 1 ¼ teaspoon cinnamon
- ¼ cup brown sugar
- ½ cup walnuts, chopped
- 3 tablespoon butter, unsalted
- 1 teaspoon salt

Directions:

1. Add all the prepared ingredients to the bread machine pan in the order recommended by your bread machine manufacturer.
2. Set bread machine to the sweet bread cycle with medium crust.
3. Once your bread is done, remove it from the bread machine pan and let it cool completely.
4. Slice and serve.

Nutritional Value: Calories 304; Fat 7g; Carbohydrates 54.4g; Protein 6.4g

Recipe 32: Bacon Basil Bread

Serving Size: 8

Cooking Time: 3 hours 10 minutes

Ingredients:

- 3 cups white flour
- 1 teaspoon bread machine yeast
- ½ cup bacon, cooked & crumbled
- ¾ cup cheddar cheese, shredded
- ½ teaspoon dried basil
- 1 tablespoon sugar
- 1 tablespoon olive oil
- 1 ¼ cups water
- 1 ½ teaspoon salt

Directions:

1. Add all the ingredients except cheese and bacon to the bread machine pan in the order recommended by your bread machine manufacturer.
2. Set bread machine to the basic bread cycle with medium crust.
3. When the machine beeps, add the cheese and bacon.
4. Once your bread is done, remove it from the bread machine pan and let it cool completely.
5. Slice and serve.

Nutritional Value: Calories 242; Fat 6.2g; Carbohydrates 37.6g; Protein 8.1g

Recipe 33: Butter Bread

Serving Size: 6

Cooking Time: 3 hours 50 minutes

Ingredients:

- 1 medium egg
- ½ cup butter
- 300 ml milk
- 1 teaspoon salt
- ½ teaspoon sugar
- 2 cups plain bread flour
- 1 teaspoon bread improver (optional)
- 1 ¾ teaspoons instant dried yeast

Directions:

1. Chop the butter into small pieces.
2. It is required to add the ingredients in your bread machine according to the bread machine's recommended order: egg, butter, milk.
3. Add the salt and sugar next—scatter them across the pan edge.
4. Then add wheat flour and bread.
5. Finally, in the flour, create a hole and put the yeast in it.
6. Use bread maker's French cycle, 1kg loaf size (this is a triple, rising setting) and medium crust. If your bread maker doesn't have this setting, use the white bread setting.
7. Take it out from the pan immediately and let the bread cool on a rack.
8. Don't slice it until the bread is completely cool and store it in the fridge after a couple of days.

Nutritional Value: Calories 180; Fat 16.4g; Carbohydrates 6.3g; Protein 2.17g

Recipe 34: Butter Honey Wheat Bread

Serving Size: 12

Cooking Time: 3 hours 45 minutes

Ingredients:

- 1 tablespoon Buttermilk
- 2 tablespoon Butter, melted
- 1 tablespoon Honey
- 2 cups Bread flour
- ¼ cup Whole-wheat flour
- ½ teaspoon Salt
- 1 tablespoon Baking soda
- 1 tbs. Active dry yeast

Directions:

1. Put all the prepared ingredients into the bread machine, by way recommended by the manufacturer.
2. In my case, liquids always go first.
3. Run the bread machine for a loaf (1½ lbs.) on the Whole Wheat setting.
4. Once the baking process is done, transfer the baked bread to a wire rack and cool before slicing.
5. Enjoy!

Nutritional Value: Calories 170; Fat 6g; Carbohydrates 27g; Protein 3g

Recipe 35: Cheddar Cheese Bread

Serving Size: 12

Cooking Time: 3 hours 40 minutes

Ingredients:

- 3 cups all-purpose flour
- 1 ¼ oz active dry yeast
- 1 tablespoon sugar
- ½ teaspoon garlic powder
- 2 cups cheddar cheese, shredded
- ½ cup butter, unsalted & melted
- 1 cup milk
- 2 teaspoon kosher salt

Directions:

1. Add all the prepared ingredients to the bread machine pan in the order recommended by your bread machine manufacturer.
2. Set bread machine to the basic bread cycle with a light crust.
3. Once your bread is actually done, remove it from the bread machine pan and let it cool completely.
4. Slice and serve.

Nutritional Value: Calories 280; Fat 14.8g; Carbohydrates 27.3g; Protein 9.8g

Recipe 36: Chia Seed Bread

Serving Size: 16

Cooking Time: 40 minutes

Ingredients:

- ½ teaspoon xanthan gum
- ½ cup butter
- 2 tablespoon coconut oil
- 1 tablespoon baking powder
- 3 tablespoon sesame seeds
- 2 tablespoon chia seeds
- ½ teaspoon salt
- ¼ cup sunflower seeds
- 2 cups almond flour
- 7 eggs

Directions:

1. Preheat the oven to 350F.
2. Beat eggs in a bowl on high for 1 to 2 minutes.
3. Beat in the xanthan gum and combine coconut oil and melted butter into eggs, beating continuously.
4. Set aside the sesame seeds, but add the rest of the ingredients.
5. Line a loaf pan with baking paper and place the mixture in it. Top the mixture with sesame seeds.
6. Bake in the prepared preheated oven until a toothpick inserted comes out clean, about 35 to 40 minutes.

Nutritional Value: Calories 405; Fat 37g; Carbohydrates 4g; Protein 14g

Recipe 37: Cinnamon Raisin Bread

Serving Size: 12

Cooking Time: 3 hours

Ingredients:

- 2 eggs, beaten
- 3 ½ cups whole wheat flour
- 2 teaspoon dry yeast
- ¼ cup butter, unsalted & softened
- ¾ cup water
- 1/3 cup milk
- 1/3 cup sugar
- 3 ½ teaspoon cinnamon
- 1 cup raisins
- 1 teaspoon salt

Directions:

1. Add all the prepared ingredients to the bread machine pan in the order recommended by your bread machine manufacturer.
2. Set bread machine to the whole wheat bread cycle with medium crust.
3. Once your bread is done, remove it from the bread machine pan and let it cool completely.
4. Slice and serve.

Nutritional Value: Calories 241; Fat 5.2g; Carbohydrates 44.1g; Protein 5.6g

Recipe 38: Cottage Cheese Bread

Serving Size: 12

Cooking Time: 3 hours 5 minutes

Ingredients:

- 1/2 cup water
- 1 cup cottage cheese
- 2 tablespoons margarine
- 1 egg
- 1 tablespoon white sugar
- 1/4 teaspoon baking soda
- 1 teaspoon salt
- 3 cups bread flour
- 2 1/2 teaspoons active dry yeast

Directions:

1. Into the bread machine, place the ingredients according to the order recommended by manufacturer and then push the start button.
2. In case the dough looks too sticky, feel free to use up to half cup more bread flour.

Nutritional Value: Calories 171; Fat 3.6g; Carbohydrates 26.8g; Protein 7.3g

Recipe 39: Cranberry Yogurt Bread

Serving Size: 8

Cooking Time: 25 minutes

Ingredients:

- 3 cups + 2 tablespoons bread or all-purpose flour
- 1/2 cup lukewarm water
- 1 tablespoon olive or coconut oil
- 1 tablespoon orange or lemon essential oil
- 3 tablespoons sugar
- 3/4 cup yogurt
- 2 teaspoons instant yeast
- 1 cup dried cried cranberries
- 1/2 cup raisins

Directions:

1. Preparing the ingredients. Place all ingredients, except cranberries and raisins, in the bread pan in the liquid-dry yeast layering.
2. Put the pan in the Hamilton Beach bread machine.
3. Load the fruits in the automatic dispenser.
4. Select the Bake cycle. Choose White bread.
5. Press start and wait until the loaf is cooked.
6. The machine will actually start the keep warm mode after the bread is complete.
7. Allow it to stay in that mode for at least 10 minutes before unplugging.
8. Remove the pan and let it cool down for about 10 minutes.

Nutritional Value: Calories 277; Fat 1.9g; Carbohydrates 48.4g; Protein 9.4g

Recipe 40: French Bread

Serving Size: 14

Cooking Time: 3 hours 40 minutes

Ingredients:

- 4 cups all-purpose flour
- 2 tablespoon sugar
- 2 teaspoon yeast
- 1 ½ tablespoon extra-virgin olive oil
- 1 1/3 cups warm water
- 1 ½ teaspoon salt

Directions:

1. Add all the prepared ingredients to the bread machine pan in the order recommended by your bread machine manufacturer.
2. Set bread machine to the French bread cycle with a light crust.
3. Once your bread is actually done, remove it from the bread machine pan and let it cool completely.
4. Slice and serve.

Nutritional Value: Calories 151; Fat 1.9g; Carbohydrates 29.2g; Protein 3.9g

Recipe 41: Garlic Bread

Serving Size: 6

Cooking Time: 15 minutes

Ingredients:

- 5 oz. beef
- 15 oz. almond flour
- 5 oz. rye flour
- 1 onion
- 3 teaspoons dry yeast
- 5 tablespoons olive oil
- 1 tablespoon sugar
- Sea salt
- Ground black pepper

Directions:

1. Pour the warm water into the 15 oz. of the wheat flour and rye flour and leave overnight.
2. Chop the onions and cut the beef into cubes.
3. Fry the onions until clear and golden brown and then mix in the bacon and fry on low heat for 20 minutes until soft.
4. Combine the yeast with the warm water, mixing until smooth consistency and then combine the yeast with the flour, salt and sugar, but don't forget to mix and knead well.
5. Add in the fried onions with the beef and black pepper and mix well.
6. Pour some oil into a bread machine and place the dough into the bread maker. Cover the prepared dough with the towel and leave for 1 hour.
7. Close the lid and turn the bread machine on the basic/white bread program.
8. Bake the bread until the medium crust and after the bread is ready take it out and leave for 1 hour covered with the towel and only then you can slice the bread.

Nutritional Value: Calories 299; Fat 21g; Carbohydrates 6g; Protein 13g

Recipe 42: Garlic Parmesan Bread

Serving Size: 12

Cooking Time: 3 hours 40 minutes

Ingredients:

- 3 ½ cups all-purpose flour
- ¼ oz active dry yeast
- 3 tablespoon sugar
- 1 teaspoon dried oregano
- 1 teaspoon dried basil
- ½ teaspoon garlic powder
- ½ cup parmesan cheese, grated
- 1 tablespoon garlic, minced
- ¼ cup butter, unsalted & melted
- 1/3 cup vegetable oil
- 1 1/3 cups water
- 2 teaspoon salt

Directions:

1. Add all the prepared ingredients to the bread machine pan in the order recommended by your bread machine manufacturer.
2. Set bread machine to the basic bread cycle with a light crust.
3. Once your bread is done, remove it from the bread machine pan and let it cool completely.
4. Slice and serve.

Nutritional Value: Calories 247; Fat 11.1g; Carbohydrates 31.6g; Protein 5.3g

Recipe 43: Golden Turmeric Cardamom Bread

Serving Size: 12

Cooking Time: 3 hours

Ingredients:

- 1 cup lukewarm water
- 1/3 cup lukewarm milk
- 3 tablespoons butter, unsalted
- 3 3/4 cups unbleached all-purpose flour
- 3 tablespoons sugar
- 1 1/2 teaspoons salt
- 2 tablespoons ground turmeric
- 1 tablespoon ground cardamom
- 1/2 teaspoon cayenne pepper
- 1 1/2 teaspoons active dry yeast

Directions:

2. Add liquid ingredients to the bread pan.
3. Measure and add dry ingredients (except yeast) to the bread pan.
4. Make a well in the actual center of the dry ingredients and add the yeast.
5. Snap the baking pan into the bread maker and close the lid.
6. Choose the Basic setting, preferred crust color and press Start.
7. When the loaf is done, remove the pan from the machine. After about 5 minutes, gently shake the pan to loosen the loaf and turn it out onto a rack to cool.

Nutritional Value: Calories 183; Fat 3.3g; Carbohydrates 33.3g; Protein 4.5g

Recipe 44: Grain Bread

Serving Size: 8

Cooking Time: 25 minutes

Ingredients:

- 1 1/3 cups warm water
- 1 tablespoon active dry yeast
- 3 tablespoons dry milk powder
- 2 tablespoons vegetable oil
- 2 tablespoons honey
- 2 teaspoons salt
- 1 egg
- 1 cup whole wheat flour
- 1/2 cups bread flour
- 3/4 cup 7-grain cereal

Directions:

1. Follow the order of putting the ingredients into the pan of the bread machine recommended by the manufacturer.
2. Choose the Whole Wheat Bread cycle on the machine and press the Start button to run the machine.

Nutritional Value: Calories 211; Fat 21g; Carbohydrates 6g; Protein 28g

Recipe 45: High Protein Bread

Serving Size: 8

Cooking Time: 25 minutes

Ingredients:

- 2 teaspoons active dry yeast
- 1 cup bread flour
- 1 cup whole-wheat flour
- ¼ cup soy flour
- ¼ cup powdered soy milk
- ¼ cup oat bran
- 1 tablespoon canola oil
- 1 tablespoon honey
- 1 teaspoon salt
- 1 cup water

Directions:

1. Into the bread machine's pan, put the ingredients by following the order suggested by the manufacturer.
2. Set the machine to either the regular setting or the basic medium.
3. Push the Start button.

Nutritional Value: Calories 137; Fat 2.4g; Carbohydrates 24.1g; Protein 6.5g

Recipe 46: Honey Oat Bread

Serving Size: 8

Cooking Time: 3 hours

Ingredients:

- 2 1/3 cups pure oat flour
- 1 cup pure rolled oats
- 2 ¼ teaspoons baking powder
- 1 ¼ teaspoons salt
- 1 teaspoon baking soda
- 1 egg
- 1 cup yoghurt, plain
- ¾ cup almond milk
- ¼ cup coconut oil
- ¼ cup honey

Directions:

1. Add all wet ingredients first in the bread pan before the dry ingredients.
2. Press the "Basic" or "Normal" mode of the bread machine.
3. Select "Medium" as the crust color setting.
4. Wait until the machine finishes the mixing, kneading, and baking cycles.
5. Take out the bread from the machine.
6. Let it cool down for about an hour before slicing.

Nutritional Value: Calories 181; Fat 7g; Carbohydrates 24g; Protein 7g

Recipe 47: Honey Wheat Bread

Serving Size: 12

Cooking Time: 3 hours 30 minutes

Ingredients:

- 4 1/2 cups 100% whole wheat flour
- 1 1/2 cups warm water
- 1/3 cup olive oil
- 1/3 cup honey
- 2 teaspoons salt
- 1 tablespoon active dry yeast

Directions:

1. Add water to the bread maker.
2. Measure and add the prepared oil first, then the honey in the same measuring cup: this will make the honey slip out of the measuring cup more easily.
3. Add salt, then flour.
4. Make a prepared small well in the flour and add the yeast.
5. Set to Wheat Bread, choose crust color, and press Start.
6. Remove and allow to actually cool on a wire rack when baked, before serving.

Nutritional Value: Calories 232; Fat 6.5g; Carbohydrates 40.8g; Protein 6.6g

Recipe 48: Honey Whole Wheat Bread

Serving Size: 10

Cooking Time: 50 minutes

Ingredients:

- 1 1/8 cups of warm water (110°F/45°C)
- 3 tablespoons honey
- ⅓ teaspoon salt
- 1 ½ cups whole-wheat flour
- 1 ½ cups bread flour
- 2 tablespoons vegetable oil
- 1 ½ teaspoons active dry yeast

Directions:

1. Place the ingredients into the bread machine following the order suggested by the manufacturer.
2. Select the Wheat Bread cycle and the setting for Light Color on the machine.

Nutritional Value: Calories 180; Fat 3.5g; Carbohydrates 33.4g; Protein 5.2g

Recipe 49: Lavender Buttermilk Bread

Serving Size: 14

Cooking Time: 3 hours

Ingredients:

- ½ cup water
- 7/8 cup buttermilk
- 1/4 cup olive oil
- 3 Tablespoon finely chopped fresh lavender leaves
- 1 ¼ teaspoon finely chopped fresh lavender flowers
- Grated zest of 1 lemon
- 4 cups bread flour
- 2 teaspoon salt
- 2 3/4 teaspoon bread machine yeast

Directions:

1. Add each ingredient to the bread machine in the order and at the temperature recommended by your bread machine manufacturer.
2. Close the lid, select the basic bread, medium crust setting on your bread machine and press start.
3. When the bread machine has finished baking, remove the bread and put it on a cooling rack.

Nutritional Value: Calories 304; Fat 21g; Carbohydrates 6g; Protein 28g

Recipe 50: Mexican Sweet Bread

Serving Size: 12

Cooking Time: 3 hours

Ingredients:

- 1 cup whole milk
- 1/4 cup butter
- 1 egg
- 1/4 cup sugar
- 1 teaspoon salt
- 3 cups bread flour
- 1 1/2 teaspoons yeast

Directions:

1. Add wet ingredients to bread maker pan.
2. Add dry ingredients, except yeast.
3. Make a well in the actual center of the dry ingredients and add the yeast.
4. Set to Sweet Bread cycle, light crust color, and press Start.
5. Remove to a cooling rack for approximately about 15 minutes before serving.

Nutritional Value: Calories 182; Fat 5.2g; Carbohydrates 29.2g; Protein 4.6g

Recipe 51: Olive Cheese Bread

Serving Size: 8

Cooking Time: 25 minutes

Ingredients:

- 1 cup milk
- 1 teaspoon minced garlic
- 1 teaspoon bread machine
- 1/3 cup chopped black olives
- 1 teaspoon salt
- 2 cups white bread flour
- 1½ tablespoons sugar
- ¾ cup (3 ounces) shredded Swiss cheese
- 1½ tablespoons melted butter
-

Directions:

1. Preparing the ingredients. Place the ingredients in your Zojirushi bread machine, tossing the flour with the cheese first.
2. Prog the machine for Regular Basic, choose light or medium crust, and press Start.
3. Next, when the loaf is done, you may remove the bucket from the machine.
4. Let the loaf cool for 5 minutes.
5. Mildly shake the pot to eliminate the loaf and turn it out onto a rack to cool.

Nutritional Value: Calories 233; Fat 21g; Carbohydrates 6g; Protein 28g

Recipe 52: Orange Bread

Serving Size: 12

Cooking Time: 3 hours

Ingredients:

- 1 egg, beaten
- 2 teaspoon active dry yeast
- 4 ¼ cups bread flour
- 3 tablespoon sugar
- 1 teaspoon orange zest, grated
- 2 tablespoon vegetable oil
- 1 3/8 cups milk
- 1 ½ teaspoon salt

Directions:

1. Add all the prepared ingredients to the bread machine pan in the order recommended by your bread machine manufacturer.
2. Set bread machine to the basic bread cycle with medium crust.
3. Once your bread is actually done, remove it from the bread machine pan and let it cool completely.
4. Slice and serve.

Nutritional Value: Calories 214; Fat 3.7g; Carbohydrates 38.5g; Protein 6.2g

Recipe 53: Paleo Bread

Serving Size: 16

Cooking Time: 3 hours 15 minutes

Ingredients:

- 4 tablespoons chia seeds
- 1 tablespoon flax meal
- 3/4 cup, plus 1 tablespoon water
- 1/4 cup coconut oil
- 3 eggs, room temperature
- 1/2 cup almond milk
- 1 tablespoon honey
- 2 cups almond flour
- 1 1/4 cups tapioca flour
- 1/3 cup coconut flour
- 1 teaspoon salt
- 1/4 cup flax meal
- 2 teaspoons cream of tartar
- 1 teaspoon baking soda
- 2 teaspoons active dry yeast

Directions:

1. Combine the prepared chia seeds and tablespoon of flax meal in a mixing bowl; stir in the water and set aside. Melt the prepared coconut oil in a microwave-safe dish, and let it cool down to lukewarm. Whisk in the eggs, almond milk and honey.
2. Whisk in the chia seeds and flax meal gel and pour it into the bread maker pan.
3. Stir the almond flour, tapioca flour, coconut flour, salt and 1/4 cup of flax meal together.
4. Mix the prepared cream of tartar and baking soda in a separate bowl and combine it with the other dry ingredients.
5. Pour the dry ingredients into the bread machine. Make a little well on top and add the yeast. Start the machine on the Wheat cycle, light or medium crust color, and press Start. Remove to cool completely before slicing to serve.

Nutritional Value: Calories 190; Fat 10.3g; Carbohydrates 20.4g; Protein 4.5g

Recipe 54: Pepperoni Cheese Bread

Serving Size: 12

Cooking Time: 3 hours

Ingredients:

- 3 ¼ cups bread flour
- 2/3 cup pepperoni, diced
- 1 ½ teaspoon active dry yeast
- 1 ½ teaspoon dried oregano
- 1 ½ teaspoon garlic salt
- 2 tablespoon sugar
- 1/3 cup mozzarella cheese, shredded
- 1 cup + 2 tablespoon warm water

Directions:

1. Add all the ingredients except pepperoni to the bread machine pan in the order recommended by your bread machine manufacturer.
2. Set bread machine to the basic bread cycle with medium crust.
3. When the machine beeps, add the pepperoni.
4. Once your bread is done, remove it from the bread machine pan and let it cool completely.
5. Slice and serve.

Nutritional Value: Calories 164; Fat 3g; Carbohydrates 28.4g; Protein 5.3g

Recipe 55: Saffron Tomato Bread

Serving Size: 10

Cooking Time: 15 minutes

Ingredients:

- 1 teaspoon bread machine yeast
- 2½ cups wheat bread machine flour
- 1 Tablespoon panifarin
- 1½ teaspoon kosher salt
- 1½ Tablespoon white sugar
- Tablespoon extra-virgin olive oil
- Tablespoon tomatoes, dried and chopped
- 1 Tablespoon tomato paste
- ½ cup firm cheese (cubes)
- ½ cup feta cheese
- 1 pinch saffron
- 1½ cups serum

Directions:

1. For 5 minutes before cooking, pour in dried tomatoes and 1 tablespoon of olive oil. Add the tomato paste and mix.
2. Place all the dry and liquid ingredients, except additives, in the pan and follow the instructions for your bread machine.
3. Pay particular attention to measuring the ingredients. Use a measuring cup, measuring spoon, and kitchen scales to do so.
4. Set the baking prog to BASIC and the crust type to MEDIUM.
5. Add the additives after the beep or place them in the dispenser of the bread machine.
6. Shake the loaf out of the pan. If necessary, use a spatula.
7. Wrap the bread with a kitchen towel and set it aside for an hour. Otherwise, you can cool it on a wire rack.

Nutritional Value: Calories 222; Fat 10g; Carbohydrates 6g; Protein 28g

Recipe 56: Semolina Bread

Serving Size: 10

Cooking Time: 3 hours 25 minutes

Ingredients:

- 4 cups semolina
- 2 tablespoon vegetable oil
- 2 tablespoon sugar
- 1 5/8 cups warm water
- 2 ¾ teaspoon active dry yeast
- 1 ¾ teaspoon salt

Directions:

1. Add water and salt into the bread machine pan.
2. Next add oil, semolina, sugar, and yeast.
3. Set bread machine to the white bread cycle with medium crust.
4. Once your bread is done, remove it from the bread machine pan and let it cool completely.
5. Slice and serve.

Nutritional Value: Calories 277; Fat 3.5g; Carbohydrates 51.5g; Protein 8.9g

Recipe 57: Soft Egg Bread

Serving Size: 8

Cooking Time: 1 hour

Ingredients:

- ½ cup plus 2 tablespoons milk
- ¼ teaspoon bread machine yeast
- 1 egg at room temperature
- 2 ½ tablespoon sugar
- 1 teaspoon salt
- 2 ½ tablespoon melted butter
- 2 cups white bread flour

Directions:

1. Put the ingredients in your machine as suggested by the manufacturer
2. Program the basic/white cycle on the bread machine, select light or medium crust and start it.
3. Take out the bucket from the device when the loaf is finished.
4. Enable the loaf to cool for 5 mins.
5. Shake the bucket softly to extract the loaf and turn it on a rack to cool it off.

Nutritional Value: Calories 189; Fat 5.5g; Carbohydrates 28.9g; Protein 5.4g

Recipe 58: Soft Spinach and Feta Bread

Serving Size: 12

Cooking Time: 2 hours

Ingredients:

- 1 cup water
- 2 teaspoons Butter
- 3 cups flour
- 1 teaspoon sugar
- 2 teaspoons instant minced onion
- 1 teaspoon salt
- 1 ¼ teaspoon Instant yeast
- 1 cup crumbled feta
- 1 cup chopped fresh spinach leaves

Directions:

1. Prepare the ingredients.
2. Add each ingredient, except the cheese and spinach, to the bread machine in the order and at the temperature recommended by your bread machine manufacturer.
3. Close the lid, select the basic bread, medium crust setting on your bread machine, and press start.
4. When only 10 minutes are left in the last kneading cycle, add the spinach and cheese.
5. When the bread machine has finished baking, remove the bread and put it on a cooling rack.

Nutritional Value: Calories 151; Fat 3.2g; Carbohydrates 25.2g; Protein 5.2g

Recipe 59: Sun Vegetable Bread

Serving Size: 8

Cooking Time: 3 hours 45 minutes

Ingredients:

- 2 cups (250 g) wheat flour
- 2 cups (250 g) whole-wheat flour
- 2 teaspoons panifarin
- 2 teaspoons yeast
- 1½ teaspoons salt
- 1 tablespoon sugar
- 1 tablespoon paprika dried slices
- 2 tablespoons dried beets
- 1 tablespoon dried garlic
- 1½ cups water
- 1 tablespoon vegetable oil

Directions:

1. Set baking prog, which should be 4 hours; crust color is Medium.
2. Be sure to look at the kneading phase of the dough, to get a smooth and soft bun.

Nutritional Value: Calories ; Fat g; Carbohydrates g; Protein g

Recipe 60: Zucchini Bread

Serving Size: 8

Cooking Time: 12 hours 40 minutes

Ingredients:

- 1/2 teaspoon salt
- 1 cup sugar
- 1 tablespoon pumpkin pie spice
- 1 tablespoon baking powder
- 1 teaspoon pure vanilla extract
- 1/3 cup milk
- 1/2 cup vegetable oil
- 2 eggs
- 2 cups bread flour
- 1 1/2 teaspoons active dry yeast or bread machine yeast
- 1 cup shredded zucchini, raw and unpeeled
- 1 cup of chopped walnuts (optional)

Directions:

1. Add all of the ingredients for the zucchini bread into the bread maker pan in the order listed above, reserving yeast.
2. Make a well in the actual center of the dry ingredients and add the yeast.
3. Select Wheat bread cycle, medium crust color, and press Start.
4. Transfer to a cooling rack for approximately about 10 to 15 minutes before slicing to serve.

Nutritional Value: Calories 304; Fat 16.4g; Carbohydrates 35.5g; Protein 6.1g

Chapter 3:   Dinner Recipes

Recipe 61: Apricot Bread

Serving Size: 12

Cooking Time: 3 hours

Ingredients:

- 1 egg
- 3 ½ cups bread flour
- 2 ¼ teaspoon active dry yeast
- 1 teaspoon lemon zest, grated
- ¼ cup butter, unsalted
- ½ cup apricots preserves
- ½ cup water
- 1 teaspoon salt

Directions:

1. Add all the prepared ingredients to the bread machine pan in the order recommended by your bread machine manufacturer.
2. Set bread machine to the basic bread cycle with a light crust.
3. Once your bread is done, remove it from the bread machine pan and let it cool completely.
4. Slice and serve.

Nutritional Value: Calories 208; Fat 4.6g; Carbohydrates 36.8g; Protein 4.6g

Recipe 62: Bacon Beer Bread

Serving Size: 12

Cooking Time: 3 hours

Ingredients:

- 3 ¼ cups bread flour
- 1/3 cup bacon, cooked & crumbled
- 1 ¾ teaspoon bread machine yeast
- 1 tablespoon sugar
- 1 tablespoon butter, unsalted & softened
- 2 tablespoon garlic mustard sauce
- ¼ cup green onions, chopped
- ½ cup warm water
- ¾ cup beer
- ¾ teaspoon sea salt

Directions:

1. Add all the ingredients except bacon to the bread machine pan in the order recommended by your bread machine manufacturer.
2. Set bread machine to the basic bread cycle with medium crust.
3. When the machine beeps, add the bacon.
4. Once your bread is done, remove it from the bread machine pan and let it cool completely.
5. Slice and serve.

Nutritional Value: Calories 149; Fat 1.7g; Carbohydrates 27.7g; Protein 4g

Recipe 63: Beer Cheese Bread

Serving Size: 10

Cooking Time: 2 hours

Ingredients:

- 4 oz. shredded Monterey Jack cheese
- 4 oz. shredded American cheese
- 10 oz. beer
- 1 tablespoon butter
- 1 tablespoon sugar
- 3 cups bread flour
- 1 packet active dry yeast
- 1 ½ teaspoon salt

Directions:

1. Place the ingredients into the pan of the bread machine.
2. Select the basic setting, then select a light crust and start.
3. Once the loaf is done, remove the loaf pan from the machine.
4. Allow it to cool for 10 mins.
5. Slice and serve.

Nutritional Value: Calories 245; Fat 7.8g; Carbohydrates 32.1g; Protein 9.2g

Recipe 64: Blue Cheese Bread

Serving Size: 12

Cooking Time: 15 minutes

Ingredients:

- ¾ cup warm water
- 1 large egg
- 1 teaspoon salt
- 3 cups bread flour
- 1 cup blue cheese, crumbled
- 2 tablespoons nonfat dry milk
- 2 tablespoons sugar
- 1 teaspoon bread machine yeast

Directions:

1. Prepare the ingredients.
2. Add the prepared ingredients to the bread machine pan in the order listed above, except yeast, be sure to add the cheese with the flour.
3. Make a well in the flour; pour the yeast into the hole.
4. Select Basic bread cycle, medium crust color and press Start.
5. When finished, transfer to a cooling rack for 10 mins and serve warm.

Nutritional Value: Calories 174; Fat 4.18g; Carbohydrates 26.5g; Protein 6.8g

Recipe 65: Brown Rice Bread

Serving Size: 12

Cooking Time: 3 hours

Ingredients:

- ⅓ cup brown rice
- 2/3 cup water
- 1 ½ tablespoon olive oil
- Warm water
- 3 cups bread flour
- 2 tablespoons white sugar
- 1 teaspoon salt
- 1 ½ teaspoons active dry yeast

Directions:

1. Boil water in a saucepan, then add rice to it and stir. Reduce heat, cover and simmer for approximately about 15 mins.
2. In a 2-measuring cup, add half a cup of cooked rice. Add warm water and oil to equal 1 ½ cups. Add this combination to the pan of the bread maker. Add salt, flour, sugar and yeast. Select the setting and start it.

Nutritional Value: Calories 141; Fat 2.4g; Carbohydrates 25.1g; Protein 4.3g

Recipe 66: Butter Up Bread

Serving Size: 12

Cooking Time: 3 hours

Ingredients:

- 1 cup bread flour
- 2 tablespoons Margarine, melted
- 2 tablespoons Buttermilk at 1100°F (450°C)
- 1 tablespoons Sugar
- 1 tablespoons Active dry yeast
- ½ teaspoons Salt

Directions:

1. Prepare the bread machine pan by adding buttermilk, melted margarine, salt, sugar, flour and yeast in the order specified by your manufacturer.
2. Select Basic/White Setting and press Start.
3. Once baked, transfer onto wire racks to cool before slicing.
4. Enjoy!

Nutritional Value: Calories 231; Fat 6g; Carbohydrates 36g; Protein 8g

Recipe 67: Cheese Pepperoni Bread

Serving Size: 10

Cooking Time: 2 hours

Ingredients:

- 2/3 cup pepperoni diced
- 1 ½ teaspoon active dry yeast
- 3 ¼ cups bread flour
- 1 ½ teaspoon dried oregano
- 1 ½ teaspoon garlic salt
- 2 tablespoons sugar
- ⅓ cup shredded mozzarella cheese
- 1 cup + 2 tablespoons warm water

Directions:

1. Add all the ingredients, except for pepperoni, into the bread machine pan.
2. Select basic setting, then selects medium crust and press start.
3. Add pepperoni just before the final kneading cycle.
4. Once the loaf is done, remove the loaf pan from the machine.
5. Allow it to cool for 10 mins.
6. Slice and serve.

Nutritional Value: Calories 176; Fat 1.5g; Carbohydrates 34.5g; Protein 5.7g

Recipe 68: Cherry Cocoa Bread

Serving Size: 12

Cooking Time: 3 hours

Ingredients:

- 3 cups bread flour
- ½ cup dried cherries
- ½ cup pecans, chopped
- 2 ¼ teaspoon active dry yeast
- 5 tablespoon cocoa powder
- 1/3 cup brown sugar
- 5 tablespoon butter, unsalted & softened
- 1/3 cup warm water
- 2/3 cup warm milk
- 1 teaspoon salt

Directions:

1. Add all the ingredients except cherries and pecans to the bread machine pan in the order recommended by your bread machine manufacturer.
2. Set bread machine to the basic bread cycle with a light crust.
3. When the machine beeps, add the dried cherries and pecans.
4. Once your bread is done, remove it from the bread machine pan and let it cool completely.
5. Slice and serve.

Nutritional Value: Calories 193; Fat 6.1g; Carbohydrates 30.9g; Protein 4.5g

Recipe 69: Cinnamon Squash Bread

Serving Size: 12

Cooking Time: 2 hours

Ingredients:

- 1 egg, beaten
- 1 cup all-purpose flour
- ¼ teaspoon nutmeg
- 1/3 cup butter, melted
- 1 teaspoon baking soda
- 1 ½ cups summer squash, grated
- 1 teaspoon vanilla
- 1 teaspoon cinnamon
- 2/3 cup sugar
- ½ cup whole wheat flour

Directions:

1. Add all the prepared ingredients to the bread machine pan in the order recommended by your bread machine manufacturer.
2. Set bread machine to the quick bread cycle with medium crust.
3. Once your bread is done, remove it from the bread machine pan and let it cool completely.
4. Slice and serve.

Nutritional Value: Calories 154; Fat 5.7g; Carbohydrates 23.9g; Protein 2.3g

Recipe 70: Cinnamon Sugar Bread

Serving Size: 12

Cooking Time: 3 hours 40 minutes

Ingredients:

- 1 egg
- 2 teaspoon yeast
- 1 ¼ teaspoon cinnamon
- ½ cup sugar
- 3 cups bread flour
- ¼ cup butter, unsalted & softened
- 1 cup milk
- ½ teaspoon salt

Directions:

1. Add all the prepared ingredients to the bread machine pan in the order recommended by your bread machine manufacturer.
2. Set bread machine to the white bread cycle with medium crust.
3. Once your bread is done, remove it from the bread machine pan and let it cool completely.
4. Slice and serve.

Nutritional Value: Calories 197; Fat 5g; Carbohydrates 33.7g; Protein 4.7g

Recipe 71: Crunchy Honey Wheat Bread

Serving Size: 12

Cooking Time: 45 minutes

Ingredients:

- 1 cup warm water at 110°F (45°C)
- 2 tablespoons Vegetable oil
- 2 tablespoons Honey
- 1 tablespoon salt
- 1 cup bread flour
- 1 cup Whole-wheat flour
- ½ cup Granola
- 2 tablespoons Active dry yeast

Directions:

1. Place the ingredients into the bread machine following the order recommended by the manufacturer.
2. Choose the Whole-Wheat setting or the dough cycle on the machine. Press the Start button.
3. Once the machine has finished the whole cycle of baking the bread in the oven, form the dough and add it into a loaf pan that's greased. Let it rise in volume in a warm place until it becomes double its size. Insert it into the preheated 350°F (175°C) oven and bake for 35-45 mins.
4. Enjoy!

Nutritional Value: Calories 199; Fat 4.2g; Carbohydrates 37g; Protein 6.2g

Recipe 72: Dark Pumpernickel Bread

Serving Size: 10

Cooking Time: 55 minutes

Ingredients:

- 1 ¼ cups water
- 1 ½ tablespoon oil
- ⅓ cup molasses
- 1 ½ teaspoon salt
- 1 ½ cups flour (bread flour)
- 1 cup flour (medium rye)
- 1 cup flour (whole wheat)
- 3 tablespoons wheat gluten
- 3 tablespoons cocoa powder
- 1 tablespoon caraway (seeds)
- 2 teaspoons yeast (active, dry)

Directions:

1. Arrange all the ingredients.
2. Place them in the pan and use a small quantity of liquid. Make sure to add the ingredients in the order mentioned. Do not mix them.
3. Place the machine's lid back.
4. Select the Medium Crust and Whole Wheat cycle settings and click the Start button.
5. Observe as it kneads the dough. If it seems to be dry after 5 to 10 mins or if the machine sounds like it's straining, add 1 tablespoon of more liquid at a time before the dough is smooth, fluffy and somewhat tacky to the touch.
6. Let the machine function, once kneaded, then let the dough rise and bake it.
7. Cool the bread for 1 hour after the baking period finishes before slicing.

Nutritional Value: Calories 218; Fat 2.8g; Carbohydrates 43.3g; Protein 5.2g

Recipe 73: Garlic, Herb and Cheese Bread

Serving Size: 12

Cooking Time: 45 minutes

Ingredients:

- ½ cup ghee
- 6 eggs
- 2 cups almond flour
- 1 teaspoon baking powder
- ½ teaspoon xanthan gum
- 1 cup cheddar cheese, shredded
- 1 tablespoon garlic powder
- 1 tablespoon parsley
- ½ tablespoon oregano
- ½ teaspoon salt

Directions:

1. Lightly beat eggs and ghee before pouring into bread machine pan.
2. Add the remaining ingredients to the pan.
3. Set bread machine to gluten free.
4. When the bread is done, remove bread machine pan from the bread machine.
5. Let cool slightly before transferring to a cooling rack.
6. You can store your bread for up to 5 days in the refrigerator.

Nutritional Value: Calories 156; Fat 13g; Carbohydrates 4g; Protein 5g

Recipe 74: Gingerbread Lemon Bread

Serving Size: 8

Cooking Time: 45 minutes

Ingredients:

- 1 cup milk.
- ¼ cup water.
- 1 egg
- 3 tablespoon margarine.
- 1 teaspoon brown sugar.
- 1¼ teaspoons dry yeast.
- ½ cup lemon peels.
- 3 tablespoon chopped ginger

Directions:

1. Choose the loaf size.
2. Add the ingredients above to the machine's baking tray.
3. Choose the basic white bread cycle.
4. Wait for the dough to get baked!

Nutritional Value: Calories 110; Fat 2g; Carbohydrates 11g; Protein 3g

Recipe 75: Honey Buttermilk Wheat Bread

Serving Size: 12

Cooking Time: 3 hours

Ingredients:

- ½ cup whole wheat flour
- 2 ½ cups bread flour
- 1 teaspoon yeast
- ¼ teaspoon baking soda
- 1 tablespoon butter, unsalted
- 2 tablespoon honey
- 1 cup + 1 tablespoon buttermilk
- ½ teaspoon salt

Directions:

1. Add all the prepared ingredients to the bread machine pan in the order recommended by your bread machine manufacturer.
2. Set bread machine to the whole wheat bread cycle with medium crust.
3. Once your bread is done, remove it from the bread machine pan and let it cool completely.
4. Slice and serve.

Nutritional Value: Calories 173; Fat 1.9g; Carbohydrates 31.8g; Protein 6.8g

Recipe 76: Mozzarella and Salami Bread

Serving Size: 8

Cooking Time: 25 minutes

Ingredients:

- 1 cup water plus 2 tablespoons
- ½ cup (2 ounces) shredded mozzarella cheese
- 2 tablespoons sugar
- 1½ teaspoons bread machine
- 1 teaspoon salt
- 1 teaspoon dried basil
- ¼ teaspoon garlic powder
- 3¼ cups white bread flour
- ¾ cup finely diced hot German salami

Directions:

1. Place the ingredients, except the salami, in your Zojirushi bread machine.
2. Program the machine for Regular Basic, select light or medium crust and press Start.
3. Add the salami when your machine signals or 5 mins before the second kneading cycle is finished.
4. You need to remove the bucket from the machine.
5. Next is by letting the loaf cool for 5 mins.
6. Gently shake the bucket to eliminate the loaf and turn it out onto a rack to cool.

Nutritional Value: Calories 174; Fat 3.1g; Carbohydrates 31.1g; Protein 5.1g

Recipe 77: Parmesan Tomato Bread

Serving Size: 8

Cooking Time: 3 hours

Ingredients:

- 2 cups bread flour
- ¼ cup sun-dried tomatoes, chopped
- 2 teaspoon yeast
- 1/3 cup parmesan cheese, grated
- 2 teaspoon dried basil
- 1 teaspoon sugar
- 2 tablespoon olive oil
- ¼ cup milk
- ½ cup water
- 1 teaspoon salt

Directions:

1. Add all the ingredients except tomatoes to the bread machine pan in the order recommended by your bread machine manufacturer.
2. Set bread machine to the white bread cycle with medium crust.
3. When the machine beeps, add the sun-dried tomatoes.
4. Once your bread is done, remove it from the bread machine pan and let it cool completely.
5. Slice and serve.

Nutritional Value: Calories 166; Fat 4.8g; Carbohydrates 25.5g; Protein 5.1g

Recipe 78: Pear Bread

Serving Size: 12

Cooking Time: 3 hours

Ingredients:

- 1 egg, beaten
- 3 cups bread flour
- 1/2 cup can pears, mashed
- ¼ cup water
- 1 teaspoon bread machine yeast
- 1 tablespoon honey
- ¾ teaspoon salt

Directions:

1. Add all the prepared ingredients to the bread machine pan in the order recommended by your bread machine manufacturer.
2. Set bread machine to the basic bread cycle with a light crust.
3. Once your bread is done, remove it from the bread machine pan and let it cool completely.
4. Slice and serve.

Nutritional Value: Calories 129; Fat 0.7g; Carbohydrates 26.5g; Protein 3.9g

Recipe 79: Pineapple Coconut Bread

Serving Size: 8

Cooking Time: 25 minutes

Ingredients:

- 6 tablespoons butter, at room temperature
- 2 eggs, at room temperature
- ½ cup coconut milk, at room temperature
- ½ cup pineapple juice, at room temperature
- 1 cup of sugar
- 1½ teaspoons coconut extract
- 2 cups all-purpose flour
- ¾ cup shredded sweetened coconut
- 1 teaspoon baking powder
- ½ teaspoon salt

Directions:

1. Preparing the ingredients. Place the butter, eggs, coconut milk, pineapple juice, sugar, and coconut extract in your Hamilton Beach bread machine.
2. Select the Bake cycle. Program the machine for Rapid bread and press Start. While the wet ingredients are mingling, stir together the flour, coconut, baking powder, and salt in a small bowl. After the first mixing is done and the machine motions, add the dry ingredients. When the loaf is done, eliminate the bucket from the machine. Let the loaf cool for 5 minutes. Slightly shake the pot to remove the loaf and turn it out onto a rack to cool.

Nutritional Value: Calories 277; Fat 1.9g; Carbohydrates 48g; Protein 9.4g

Recipe 80: Pita Bread

Serving Size: 8

Cooking Time: 15 minutes

Ingredients:

- 2 cups almond flour, sifted
- ½ cup water
- 2 Tablespoon olive oil
- Salt, to taste
- 1 teaspoon black cumin

Directions:

1. Preheat the oven to 400F.
2. Combine the flour with salt. Add the water and olive oil.
3. Knead the dough and let stand for 15 minutes.
4. Shape the dough into 8 balls.
5. Line a baking sheet with parchment paper and flatten the balls into 8 thin rounds.
6. Sprinkle black cumin.
7. Bake for 15 minutes, serve.

Nutritional Value: Calories 173; Fat 6.9g; Carbohydrates 1.6g; Protein 1.6g

Recipe 81: Potato Bread

Serving Size: 8

Cooking Time: 45 minutes

Ingredients:

- 1 ¾ teaspoon active dry yeast
- 2 tablespoons dry milk
- ¼ cup instant potato flakes
- 2 tablespoons sugar
- 4 cups bread flour
- 1 ¼ teaspoon salt
- 2 tablespoons butter
- 1 cups water

Directions:

1. Put all the liquid ingredients in the pan. Add all the dry ingredients, except the yeast. Form a shallow hole in the middle of the dry ingredients and place the yeast.
2. Secure the pan in the machine and close the lid. Choose the Basic setting and your desired color of the crust. Press Start.
3. Allow the bread to cool before slicing.

Nutritional Value: Calories 135; Fat 0g; Carbohydrates 19g; Protein 4g

Recipe 82: Pumpkin and Sunflower Seed Bread

Serving Size: 8

Cooking Time: 25 minutes

Ingredients:

- 1 (.25 ounce) package instant yeast
- 1 cup warm water
- ¼ cup honey
- 4 teaspoons vegetable oil
- 2 cups whole-wheat flour
- ¼ cup wheat bran (optional)
- 1 teaspoon salt
- ⅓ cup sunflower seeds
- ⅓ cup shelled, toasted, chopped pumpkin seeds

Directions:

1. Into the bread machine, put the ingredients according to the order suggested by the manufacturer.
2. Next is setting the machine to the whole wheat setting, then press the start button.
3. You can add the pumpkin and sunflower seeds at the beep if your bread machine has a signal for nuts or fruit.

Nutritional Value: Calories 148; Fat 4.8g; Carbohydrates 24.1g; Protein 5.1g

Recipe 83: Pumpkin Cranberry Bread

Serving Size: 12

Cooking Time: 4 hours

Ingredients:

- ¾ cup water
- 2/3 cup canned pumpkin
- 3 tablespoon brown sugar
- 2 tablespoon vegetable oil
- 2 cups all-purpose flour
- 1 cup whole-wheat flour
- 1¼ teaspoon salt
- ½ cup sweetened dried cranberries
- ½ cup walnuts, chopped
- 1¾ teaspoon active dry yeast

Directions:

1. Place all the ingredients in the baking pan of the bread machine in the order recommended by the manufacturer.
2. Place the baking pan in the bread machine and close the lid. Select the Basic setting, press the Start button.
3. Carefully, remove the baking pan from the machine and then invert the bread loaf onto a wire rack to cool completely before slicing.
4. With a prepared sharp knife, cut the bread loaf into desired-sized slices and serve.

Nutritional Value: Calories 199; Fat 6g; Carbohydrates 31.4g; Protein 5.6g

Recipe 84: Ricotta Bread

Serving Size: 14

Cooking Time: 20 minutes

Ingredients:

- 3 tablespoons skim milk
- 2/3 cup ricotta cheese
- 4 teaspoons unsalted butter, softened to room temperature
- 1 large egg
- 2 tablespoons granulated sugar
- ½ teaspoons salt
- 1 ½ cups bread flour, + more flour, as needed
- 1 teaspoon active dry yeast

Directions:

1. Prepare the ingredients.
2. Add each ingredient to the bread machine in the order and at the temperature recommended by your bread machine manufacturer.
3. Close the lid, select the basic bread, medium crust setting on your bread machine and press start.
4. When the bread machine has finished baking, remove the bread and put it on a cooling rack.

Nutritional Value: Calories 123; Fat 2.9g; Carbohydrates 19.1g; Protein 5.1g

Recipe 85: Rosemary and Garlic Coconut Flour Bread

Serving Size: 8

Cooking Time: 45 minutes

Ingredients:

- 1/2 cup Coconut flour
- 1 stick margarine (8 tablespoon)
- 6 enormous eggs
- 1 teaspoon heating powder
- 2 teaspoon Dried Rosemary
- 1/2-1 teaspoon garlic powder
- 1/2 teaspoon Onion powder
- 1/4 teaspoon Pink Himalayan Salt

Directions:

1. Join dry fixings (coconut flour, heating powder, onion, garlic, rosemary, and salt) in a bowl and put in a safe spot.
2. Add 6 eggs to a different bowl and beat with a hand blender until you get see rises at the top.
3. Soften the stick of margarine in the microwave and gradually add it to the eggs as you beat with the hand blender.
4. When wet and dry fixings are completely consolidated in isolated dishes, gradually add the dry fixings to the wet fixings as you blend in with the hand blender.
5. Oil an 8x4 portion dish and empty the blend into it equitably.
6. Heat at 350 for 40-50 minutes (time will change contingent upon your broiler).
7. Let it rest for 10 minutes before expelling from the container. Cut up and appreciate it with spread or toasted!

Nutritional Value: Calories 398; Fat 4.7g; Carbohydrates 44.2g; Protein 0.5g

Recipe 86: Rum Butter Bread

Serving Size: 12

Cooking Time: 3 hours

Ingredients:

- 1 egg
- 3 tablespoon brown sugar
- 3 cups bread flour
- 3 tablespoon butter, softened
- 1 tablespoon rum extract
- ¼ teaspoon nutmeg
- 1 teaspoon bread machine yeast
- ¼ teaspoon cardamom
- ½ teaspoon cinnamon
- 1 ¼ teaspoon salt

Directions:

1. Add all the prepared ingredients to the bread machine pan in the order recommended by your bread machine manufacturer.
2. Set bread machine to the basic bread cycle with medium crust.
3. Once your bread is done, remove it from the bread machine pan and let it cool completely.
4. Slice and serve.

Nutritional Value: Calories 157; Fat 3.6g; Carbohydrates 26.4g; Protein 3.9g

Recipe 87: Soft Honey Oatmeal Bread

Serving Size: 8

Cooking Time: 2 hours

Ingredients:

- 2 ½ cups bread flour
- 1 ¾ teaspoon active dry yeast
- ½ cup quick cook oats
- 1 tablespoon butter, unsalted
- 1 ½ tablespoon honey
- 8 oz warm water
- 1 teaspoon salt

Directions:

1. Add all the prepared ingredients to the bread machine pan in the order recommended by your bread machine manufacturer.
2. Set bread machine to the basic bread cycle with medium crust.
3. Once your bread is done, remove it from the bread machine pan and let it cool completely.
4. Slice and serve.

Nutritional Value: Calories 180; Fat 2.1g; Carbohydrates 35.2g; Protein 4.8g

Recipe 88: Soft Oatmeal Bread

Serving Size: 12

Cooking Time: 3 hours

Ingredients:

- 1-½ cups water (70°F to 80°C)
- ¼ cup canola oil
- 1 teaspoon lemon juice
- ¼ cup sugar
- 2 teaspoons salt
- 3 cups all-purpose flour
- 1-½ cups quick-cooking oats
- 2-½ teaspoons active dry yeast

Directions:

1. Place all the ingredients in the order proposed by the manufacturer in the bread machine pan. Select the basic setting for the bread. If available, choose the crust color and loaf size.
2. Bake as per bread machine instructions (after 5 min., observe the bread, add flour or 1-2 tablespoon water if needed).
3. Securely wrap the cooled loaf in foil and then freeze it. To use it, thaw at room temperature.

Nutritional Value: Calories 174; Fat 5.1g; Carbohydrates 27.8g; Protein 3.7g

Recipe 89: Spinach and Feta Bread

Serving Size: 14

Cooking Time: 2 hours

Ingredients:

- 1 cup water
- 2 teaspoons butter
- 3 cups flour
- 1 teaspoon sugar
- 2 teaspoons instant minced onion
- 1 teaspoon salt
- 1 ¼ teaspoons instant yeast
- 1 cup crumbled feta
- 1 cup chopped fresh spinach leaves

Directions:

1. Prepare the ingredients.
2. Add each ingredient, except the cheese and spinach, to the bread machine in the order and at the temperature recommended by your bread machine manufacturer.
3. Close the lid, select the basic bread, medium crust setting on your bread machine and press start.
4. When only 10 mins are left in the last kneading cycle, add the spinach and cheese.
5. When the bread machine has finished baking, remove the bread and put it on a cooling rack.

Nutritional Value: Calories 151; Fat 3.2g; Carbohydrates 25.2g; Protein 5.2g

Recipe 90: Whole Wheat Raisin Bread

Serving Size: 10

Cooking Time: 2 hours

Ingredients:

- 3 ½ cups Whole-wheat flour
- 2 teaspoons dry yeast
- 2 lightly beaten Eggs
- ¼ cup butter, softened
- ¾ cup Water
- ⅓ cup Milk
- 1 teaspoon Salt
- ⅓ cup Sugar
- 4 teaspoons Cinnamon
- 1 cup Raisins

Directions:

1. Add water, milk, butter and eggs to the bread pan.
2. Add the remaining ingredients except for yeast to the bread pan.
3. Make a small hole into the flour with your finger and add yeast to the hole. Make sure the yeast will not be mixed with any liquids.
4. Select the whole wheat setting, then select light/medium crust and start.
5. Once the loaf is done, remove the loaf pan from the machine. Allow it to cool for 10 mins. Slice and serve.

Nutritional Value: Calories 290; Fat 6.2g; Carbohydrates 53.1g; Protein 6.8g

Chapter 4:   Dessert Recipes

Recipe 91: Blueberry Bread

Serving Size: 12

Cooking Time: 1 hour 30 minutes

Ingredients:

- 1/2 cup blueberries
- 2 cups almond flour, blanched
- 1/2 cup Erythritol sweetener
- 2 tablespoons coconut flour
- 1 teaspoon vanilla extract, unsweetened
- 1 1/2 teaspoon baking powder
- 3 tablespoons butter, unsalted, softened
- 5 eggs, pastured
- 3 tablespoons heavy whipping cream, grass-fed, full-fat

Directions:

1. Switch on the oven, set it to 350 degrees F and let preheat.
2. Meanwhile, add vanilla in a bowl along with sweetener and eggs, whisk using an immersion blender until frothy, and then whisk in the cream until combined.
3. Place remaining ingredients in another bowl, except for butter and berries, stir until mixed, then slowly mix into egg mixture until incorporated and fold in berries until combined.
4. Take a 9 by 5 inches loaf pan, grease it with butter, pour in prepared batter and bake for 45 to 50 minutes or until the bread has cooked and an inserted toothpick into the bread comes out clean.
5. Let bread cool in its pan for 10 minutes, then take it out to cool completely on a wire rack, cut the bread into 12 slices and serve.

Nutritional Value: Calories 175; Fat 15g; Carbohydrates 3g; Protein 6g

Recipe 92: Cherry and Almond Bread

Serving Size: 8

Cooking Time: 4 hours

Ingredients:

- 1 cup milk, lukewarm
- ½ cup butter, unsalted, softened
- 2 eggs, at room temperature
- 2 cups bread flour
- 6 oz. dried cherries
- 1 cup slivered almonds, toasted
- ½ teaspoon salt
- 0.25 oz. dry yeast, active
- 1 cup sugar

Directions:

1. Gather all the ingredients needed for the bread.
2. Power on bread machine that has about 2 pounds of the bread pan.
3. Add all the ingredients in the order mentioned in the ingredients list into the bread machine pan.
4. Press the "Dough" button, key the left button, and let the mixture knead for 5 to 10 minutes.
5. Then select the "basic/white" down arrow to set baking time to 4 hours, select light or medium color for the crust, and press the start button.
6. Then prudently lift out the bread and put it on a wire rack for 1 hour or more until cooled.
7. Cut bread into sixteen slices and then serve.

Nutritional Value: Calories 125; Fat 3g; Carbohydrates 20.4g; Protein 4g

Recipe 93: Chocolate Chip Coconut Bread

Serving Size: 12

Cooking Time: 1 hour 5 minutes

Ingredients:

- 1 cup milk.
- 3 tablespoon water.
- 1 egg
- 1½ teaspoons vanilla
- 4 teaspoons margarine.
- 4 cups of bread flour.
- 3 tablespoon sugar.
- 1 teaspoon salt.
- 1¼ teaspoons active dry yeast.
- ½ cup chocolate pieces.
- ½ cup toasted coconut.

Directions:

1. Choose the loaf size.
2. Add the prepared ingredients to the machine according to the manufacturer's instructions.
3. Choose the basic white bread cycle.
4. Leave the dough to bake.

Nutritional Value: Calories 144; Fat 4g; Carbohydrates 14g; Protein 4g

Recipe 94: Chocolate Chip Peanut Butter Banana Bread

Serving Size: 8

Cooking Time: 20 minutes

Ingredients:

- 2 bananas, mashed
- 2 eggs, at room temperature
- ½ cup melted butter, cooled
- 2 tablespoons milk, at room temperature
- 1 teaspoon pure vanilla extract
- 2 cups all-purpose flour
- ½ cup sugar
- 1¼ teaspoons baking powder
- ½ teaspoon baking soda
- ½ teaspoon salt
- ½ cup peanut butter chips
- ½ cup semisweet chocolate chips

Directions:

1. Stir together the bananas, eggs, butter, milk and vanilla in the bread machine bucket and set it aside.
2. In a prepared medium bowl, toss together the flour, sugar, baking powder, baking soda, salt, peanut butter chips and chocolate chips.
3. Add the dry ingredients to the bucket.
4. Program the machine for Quick/Rapid bread and press Start.
5. When the cake is made, stick a knife into it, and if it arises out clean, the loaf is done.
6. If the loaf needs a few more minutes, look at the management panel for a Bake Only button, and extend the time by 10 mins.
7. When the loaf is done, remove the bucket from the machine.
8. Let the loaf cool for 5 mins.
9. Gently rock the can to remove the bread and turn it out onto a rack to cool.

Nutritional Value: Calories 297; Fat 14g; Carbohydrates 40g; Protein 4g

Recipe 95: Chocolate Sour Cream Bread

Serving Size: 12

Cooking Time: 10 minutes

Ingredients:

- 1 cup sour cream
- 2 eggs, at room temperature
- 1 cup sugar
- ½ cup (1 stick) butter, at room temperature
- ¼ cup plain Greek yogurt
- 1¾ cups all-purpose flour
- ½ cup unsweetened cocoa powder
- ½ teaspoon baking powder
- ½ teaspoon salt
- 1 cup milk chocolate chips

Directions:

1. In a small bowl, stick together the sour cream, eggs, sugar, butter and yogurt until just combined.
2. Transfer the wet ingredients to the bread machine bucket, and then add the flour, cocoa powder, baking powder, salt and chocolate chips.
3. Program the machine for Quick/Rapid bread and press Start.
4. When the loaf is done, stick a knife into it, and if it comes out clean, the loaf is done.
5. If the loaf needs a few more minutes, check the control panel for a Bake Only button and extend the time by 10 mins.
6. When the loaf is done, remove the bucket from the machine.
7. Let the loaf cool for 5 mins.
8. Gently rock the can to remove the loaf and place it out onto a rack to cool.

Nutritional Value: Calories 347; Fat 16g; Carbohydrates 48g; Protein 6g

Recipe 96: Chocolate Zucchini Bread

Serving Size: 10

Cooking Time: 20 minutes

Ingredients:

- 2 cups grated zucchini; excess moisture removed
- 2 eggs
- 1 tablespoon olive oil
- ⅓ cup low-carb sweetener
- 1 teaspoon vanilla extract
- ⅓ cup coconut flour
- ¼ cup unsweetened cocoa powder
- ½ teaspoon baking soda
- ½ teaspoon salt
- ⅓ cup sugar-free chocolate chips

Directions:

1. Preheat the oven to 350°F.
2. Grease the baking pan and line the entire pan with parchment paper.
3. In a food processor, blend the eggs, zucchini, oil, sweetener and vanilla.
4. Add the flour, cocoa, baking soda and salt to the zucchini mixture and stir until mixed. For a few seconds, let the batter sit.
5. Mix in the chocolate chips, then dispense the batter into the prepared pan.
6. Bake for 45 to 50 mins.
7. Cool, slice and serve.

Nutritional Value: Calories 149; Fat 8g; Carbohydrates 7g; Protein 3g

Recipe 97: Date Delight Bread

Serving Size: 12

Cooking Time: 15 minutes

Ingredients:

- ¾ cup water, lukewarm
- ½ cup milk, lukewarm
- 2 tablespoons butter
- ¼ cup honey
- 1 ½ teaspoon instant or bread machine yeast
- 3 tablespoons molasses
- 1 tablespoon sugar
- 2 ¼ cups whole-wheat flour
- 1 ¼ cups white bread flour
- 2 tablespoons skim milk powder
- 1 teaspoon salt
- 1 tablespoon unsweetened cocoa powder
- 3/4 cup chopped dates

Directions:

1. Take 1 ½ pound size loaf pan, add the liquid ingredients, and then add the dry ingredients. (Do not add the dates as of now.)
2. Place the loaf pan in the machine and close its top lid. Plug the bread machine into the power socket. For selecting a bread cycle, press "Basic Bread/White Bread/Regular Bread" or "Fruit/Nut Bread," and for choosing a crust type, press "Light" or "Medium."
3. Start the machine, and it will start preparing the bread. When the machine beeps or signals, add the dates.
4. After the bread loaf is completed, open the lid and take out the loaf pan.
5. Allow the pan to cool down for 10-15 minutes on a wire rack. Gently shake the pan and remove the bread loaf. Make slices and serve.

Nutritional Value: Calories 220; Fat 5g; Carbohydrates 52g; Protein 3g

Recipe 98: Peaches and Butter Cream Bread

Serving Size: 8

Cooking Time: 25 minutes

Ingredients:

- 3/4 cup canned peaches, drained and chopped
- 1/3 cup heavy whipping cream
- 2 1/4tablespoons sugar
- 1 1/8 teaspoons salt
  1 tablespoon melted butter cooled
- 1/3 teaspoon ground cinnamon
- 1/8 teaspoon ground nutmeg
- 1/3 cup whole-wheat flour
- 1 egg, at room temperature
-
- 2 2/3 cups white bread flour
- 1 1/6 teaspoons bread machine or instant yeast

Directions:

1. Preparing the ingredients. Place the ingredients in your Hamilton Beach bread machine.
2. Select the Bake cycle. Program the machine for Whitbread, select light or medium crust, and press Start.
3. When the loaf is done, eliminate the bucket from the machine.
4. Let the loaf cool for 5 minutes.
5. Shake the bucket to eliminate the loaf, and place it out onto a rack to cool.

Nutritional Value: Calories 277; Fat 1.9g; Carbohydrates 48.4g; Protein 9.4g

Recipe 99: Peanut Butter and Jelly Bread

Serving Size: 8

Cooking Time: 1 hour 10 minutes

Ingredients:

- 1 ½ tablespoon vegetable oil
- 1 cup water
- ½ cup blackberry jelly
- ½ cup peanut butter
- 1 teaspoon salt
- 1 tablespoon white sugar
- 2 cups bread flour
- 1 cup whole-wheat flour
- 1 ½ teaspoons active dry yeast

Directions:

1. Put everything in your bread machine pan.
2. Select the basic setting.
3. Press the start button.
4. Take out the pan when done and set it aside for 10 mins.

Nutritional Value: Calories 153; Fat 9g; Carbohydrates 20g; Protein 4g

Recipe 100: Sweet Orange and Raisins Bread

Serving Size: 6

Cooking Time: 20 minutes

Ingredients:

- 5 oz. orange zest, minced
- 5 oz. raisins
- 4 oz. macadamia nuts, ground
- 5 oz. wheat flour
- 3 eggs
- 3 teaspoons baking powder
- 6 oz. brown sugar
- 2 oz. sugar

Directions:

1. Place the raisins into the warm water and leave for 20 mins.
2. In a bowl, combine the sifted wheat flour, baking powder, brown sugar and vanilla.
3. Add the raisins, orange zest and nuts and mix well.
4. Whisk the eggs with the sugar until they have a smooth and creamy consistency.
5. Combine the eggs mixture with the flour and raisins-nuts mixture.
6. Pour the dough into the bread machine, close the lid and turn the bread machine on the basic/white bread program.
7. Bake the bread until the medium crust and, after the bread is ready, take it out and leave it for 1 hour covered with the towel and only then you can slice the bread.

Nutritional Value: Calories 154; Fat 9g; Carbohydrates 13g; Protein 7.8g

8. Conclusion

A bread maker is a valuable kitchen appliance that allows you to quickly and effortlessly prepare and serve warm, fresh, and tasty homemade bread from the comfort of your own home. A bread machine comprises a built-in bread pan and paddles that are placed in the middle of a compact and manageable multi-purpose oven. This compact oven comes with a built-in microcomputer, which is used to control the bread maker. Depending on the sort of bread you want to bake, the bread maker has multiple settings. White bread, whole wheat bread, French bread, and basic dough like pizza dough are among the options. The bread machine also has a timed setting that automatically turns on and off even if you are not nearby to operate it.

Bread machines are now created by a dozen different companies and come in dozens of versions, each with its own set of settings, functions and sizes. They're not only simple to use, but they also motivate you to create your baking cycles, resulting in bread with thin, crisp crusts and even soft-textured crumbs that rival store loaves and even some bakeries. Baking bread in a bread machine takes so little time that you can experience the luxury of fresh bread every day, as it should be.

The bread machine has actually won over many people who were previously adept at baking by hand, as well as those who were not motivated to learn how to prepare bread using an earlier approach. They were introduced to the evocative aroma, taste, and texture of baked bread through the bread machine and are now hooked.

Additives, colorants, preservatives, and chemical fixatives are all absent from homemade bread. The bread machine gives you complete control over what goes into your bread, and you can almost always count on it to be of high quality. While handcrafted loaves have a pleasing visual appeal, each machine-baked loaf is the same form as its baking pan.

Loaves of bread are generally defined in baking by the type of flour used, whether they contain yeast or not, their shape, and any additional flavorings, all of which contribute to the bread's unique personality. The recipes in this book vary in these ways, with something for every type of baker— an astonishing diversity of loaves of bread ranging from easy and familiar to innovative and demanding. There is bread for health-conscious individuals, sweet-toothed individuals, and even gluten-free individuals. Bread using familiar and unfamiliar ingredients, imaginative flatbreads, and even artisan bread employing classic techniques adapted for the bread machine is included.

This book has 400 recipes for your bread machine. Even if you are not an expert, a bread machine makes it easy to make and enjoy homemade bread. After just a few loaves in the bread machine, you'll be confident that you're a skilled baker, and you'll be pleased to discover that your loaves are ideal for serving with meals, making sandwiches or toast, or using in other recipes.

9. Index

Printed in Great Britain
by Amazon

15388032R00063